50 Special Event Ideas

To Build Business and Drive Traffic to Your Tea Room

by Amy Lawrence

Published by:
ATR Publishing

Cover Photos by:
Rob Macklin
Patrick Lawrence

Back Cover Photo by:
Sirlin Photographers
(916)444-8464
http://www.sirlin.com/

Copyright © 2010 ATR Publishing

All rights reserved. No part of this publication may be reproduced in any form or by any means, electronic or mechanical, including photocopy and information storage and retrieval system, without permission in writing from the author.

TABLE OF CONTENTS

Foreword 5

Background 7

The Idea of Opening a Tea Room 9

Chapter 1 13

   Why Are Special Events Critical to Your Business? 13

Chapter 2 19

   Key Strategies for Boosting Attendance to Your Events 19

      The Benefit of Pre-Pay Events 22

      Discount for Booking Early 23

      Other Key Strategy Ideas for Boosting Attendance to Your Event 24

Chapter 3 29

   Know Your Target Audience and Design Events around Them 29

      Experiment with Other Target Groups 30

      Cross Promote with Other Industries 33

      Other Ideas for Experimenting with Other Target Groups 35

Chapter 4 37
    How to Create Your Own Calendar of Events for the Year 37

Chapter 5 41
    Ideas to Make Your Event More Memorable 41

Chapter 6 45
    50 Special Event Ideas 45
        Anniversary Tea 45
        Children's Events 47
        Other Fun Teas for Children 49
        Tips on Planning a Children's Event 52
        Classes As Events 53
        Other Ideas for Classes 56
        Tea Tastings and Classes As Events 58
        Other Special Event Ideas 62
        Mix It Up! 63
        Above All, Have Fun! 64

About the Author 67

FOREWORD

When I started my tea room, there were hardly any resources for tea room owners. Therefore, I am dedicating this book to all of you tea room owners – present and future. It can be very lonely and scary when you open a tea room. You wear many hats and people (including your staff) expect you to know everything. Everyone depends on you. Maybe you've owned a business before, but I find that most tea room owners have not. This is all new territory for us. And yes, I did my research before I opened. I wrote a very detailed business plan. I visited every tea room I could. I even worked at another tea room for a short time before I opened mine. In addition, I read everything under the sun I could about starting a business. But the truth is, when you actually start your tea room, you are scared to death. You are afraid of failure and of being judged for not knowing everything. So when I came across a resource that mentioned a "tea room business", my heart lifted. It was like, "Ahhhh, they understand my situation. Maybe I'll find a nugget of inspiration or help here." That's why

I wrote this book for you and why I feel compelled to continue to write more resources for you. I know that's what you need. You need someone to understand your situation, give you helpful guidance and reaffirm what you are doing right.

With that said, I hope you enjoy my book. Everything in this book may not work for you, but hopefully at least it will give you some ideas and inspiration so that you can create even better events. Just know, you are doing a fabulous job! Tea rooms are all about building connections with people and the fact that you are reading this book tells me you're interested in developing a better connection with your customers. You're on the right track! I wish you the best of luck and success with your tea room! Happy reading!

-Amy Lawrence

BACKGROUND

Before I opened my tea room, An Afternoon to Remember, I had always enjoyed cooking. I remember in the 5th grade, my neighbor Ginny Lacy gave me a Junior Cookbook. She always took an interest in my wanting to learn to cook as did my grandmother, Alice Mc Coy. My mother was definitely a supporter of my cooking as she did not enjoy cooking herself. She let me have free rein of the kitchen and was happy to do dishes.

From an early age I was always enthralled with my parent's social life. My dad was an officer in the U.S. Army and with his promotions came increased social obligations. My mom would tell me about the parties and balls they would attend. Often times she was in charge of these events or at least was on the committee that planned them. I remember many times hand-writing invitations and place cards in calligraphy for a special event. I took pride in creating each one of them. At the time I was too young to attend, but my mother would return home after the special event and describe everything in detail. I especially enjoyed hearing about the food they ate.

My love for entertaining began when my father became a battalion commander in Germany. My parents would often have an open house or party at their home. Sometimes the guest list would number over 100! I enjoyed planning every detail of the menu. Appetizers and desserts were my favorites to prepare.

At this point I was in college and was also invited to attend other military functions and parties. I remember being totally enamored one New Year's Eve party with the food. One appetizer in particular was just divine! I was too embarrassed to ask the hostess for the recipe, but I did ask about the ingredients. I then promptly came home and recreated it based on my mental notes. I think it was then that I discovered I didn't need a recipe anymore. It opened my mind to create my own recipes based on what I felt would be a great dish. Little did I know then I would go on to publish 8 cookbooks.

THE IDEA OF OPENING A TEA ROOM

I am often asked, "How did you get the idea to open a tea room?" "Has it always been your childhood dream?" I think everyone is quite shocked when I tell them that it was a spur of the moment idea that just came to me out of the blue as I am not a spur of the moment person by any means.

Since the 3rd grade, I wanted to become a special education teacher. I graduated high school, went to college, got my B.S. in Education and continued straight on to get my M.S. in Special Education. In Kansas where I lived at the time, I couldn't teach special education without a M.S. I taught learning handicapped students for a few years and eventually moved to California where I taught severely handicapped students – mainly autistic students. Overall I taught for 11 years. I thoroughly enjoyed it but eventually wanted to be home with my two boys. So I took two years off and stayed at home. While I loved being home, I was restless. I often thought, "What's next?" "What else could I do?" One day my mother was visiting from Missouri. We went to tea at the Elegant Garden in Citrus Heights (sadly this tea room is now closed), I remember telling my mom, "I want to open a tea room. I love to cook. I was an assistant manager of a gift shop in high school and college. This would combine two things I love – cooking and selling gifts." I think my mom probably thought I was nuts, but she didn't say much – just supported me as she always does. That's how it all began. I had no experience other than retail. I just had a passion and a drive to succeed.

In November of 2002, I attended my first tea conference, became a certified tea consultant and finished my business plan. In January of 2003, I rented a quaint old building in Newcastle, California. It took forever to get permits to start construction on the commercial kitchen but with the help of dedicated family and friends, I finally opened my tea room on August 27, 2003. An Afternoon to Remember won many awards including Best Small Tea Room in the U.S. in 2006, KCRA's A-List 2007, 2008, 2009 and

Sacramento Magazine's Best Tea Room in 2008. Also during that time I published a cookbook every year and now have a total of 9 books.

After 6 years, I closed the tea room in June of 2009. Many people ask me why I closed. There are many reasons but the main one is my family. Owning a tea room consumes your life and although I loved the tea room, I was ready to spend more time at home. I have learned that I can't do it all, so I need to do what's most important to me.

I'm very happy with my decision to close and I stay very busy with my other companies – Afternoon to Remember Fine Tea and Gifts and ATR Publishing and I have a new one sprouting soon!

CHAPTER 1

Why Are Special Events Critical to Your Business?

Special events are crucial to your tea room business. Customers expect to be dazzled, entertained and taken back perhaps to another place in time. When I owned my tea room, my mission was to provide, "An Afternoon to Remember." You can't just do that with ordinary days. Special events are a must! People expect it and demand it.

However, after 6 years of owning and operating a tea room, I have discovered exactly why special events are critical and how valuable they really are. Even a year later after my tea room has closed, I continue to reap the benefits of my special events. Because you see, once you build a connection with your customers, you will have that connection for life. And even though my tea room isn't open any longer, any class I teach or event I do with another company, I have loyal followers. That is the single most important reason you hold events – to build that connection. Connections build customers and sales for life. Events build a connection between you and your customer.

Build and Sustain Business

Special events build and sustain business. Customers will often bring friends to events which increases business by growing your base.

Special events bring in customers, new and old, especially during the slow times. They keep customers coming back for more and they give customers a "reason" to come in. Many times customers would love to visit every week, but they can't quite justify it. If they have an event or class, it gives them a reason to come in. The great thing about special events is that you, the tea room owner, control when they happen. You can schedule events exactly when you need them. If you have a slow season, that's the time to organize a special event. Entice your customers to walk through your doors and spend money on your products.

Keep the Morale of the Staff High

Hosting special events brings excitement and variety to the normal day. Not only do your customers get bored with the same old thing, but so do your employees. Many times my staff would say, "Let's try this...." Employees love contributing to the planning of special events. They bring new ideas to the table plus they are enthusiastic in telling the customer about the event. This helps to build excitement in your tea room. Excitement is contagious and that's exactly the energy you want for your business. When people are excited, they tell others and word gets around that your tea room is "the" place to be.

Provide Content

Special events also provide content for your newsletter or other customer communications. This in turn increases the frequency of your newsletters, updates, and e-zines. After I started doing more events and classes, I never ran out of content for my newsletter and most of the time I had a hard time fitting it all in. Customers look forward to reading about your news and happenings. Even if they can't come to your event, they still get excited about it and often tell others. Events keep your business fresh, energized and full of life.

Should Special Events Always Cost the Customer?

My answer is no. If you give it away, it will come back to you. This definitely applies in the tea room world. If you make some of your events free, you will gain new customers and create new excitement. Customers often spend more when they haven't paid for the event on the same day, so you need to consider your objective. It's good to mix it up a bit – some paid events, some free.

One example of a free event I held, was an evening tea tasting with James Norwood Pratt. Although he is well-known in the tea world, in the tea room customer world he is less so. I wanted to introduce him to my customers so they would learn to appreciate the all the nuances of tea. I wanted them to be fascinated and taken with his speaking the way I am. However, I knew that if I charged for the event,

I would not have as many participants. As this was my first time having him speak at my tea room and I wanted to show him a great turn out. I advertised highly in my newsletter, e-zines and also by word of mouth to my customers. In addition, the staff was very excited about his visit even though many of them had never met him. But because I was excited, they became excited and really talked up the event. Although I made the event free, customers needed to reserve a spot. We offered a few cookies and desserts but nothing heavy as I wanted them to really "taste" the tea without the flavor of the food. In addition we sampled about 6 teas, giving each of them a small tasting cup to sample. As it turned out we ended up with over 75 people in two seatings. I was very pleased with the turnout. The customers were enthralled just like I knew they would be and they ended up buying lots of tea. The event was a success on many levels.

Because the customers had such a fabulous time, they told their friends and families. When he came to speak again in the spring, we ended up with even more people as they brought guests. So my original "free" event turned into 2 very profitable evenings.

CHAPTER 2

Key Strategies for Boosting Attendance to Your Events

It's important to get all your "ducks in a row" when you are planning for an event. I don't know how many times I have sent out an e-mail with all of the event info and then remembered a day later, "Oh no! I forgot to put it on the website." So it's good to have a system and even a checklist.

Here's what I recommend:

- Plan it on your calendar; make sure key staff will be there for the event
- Put it on your website
- Get the media involved if at all possible
- Send out an e-mail
- Send out an e-mail reminder
- Post it in your tea room, on the front door, near the cash register and other high-traffic spots (Yes, that includes the bathroom!) Some people make signs for

the table – I didn't, but it might appeal to some.
- Post it on Facebook, Twitter and other social networking sites.
- Tell your staff to promote it while serving tea or ringing up customers.
- Remind them often – at least 2 weeks before, then a week before and even a day before the event.

Stock-Up on Merchandise You Can Sell at the Event

This is a big part of the preparation process. Make sure you order merchandise early enough. I've paid for expedited shipping many times because I really needed the merchandise to be there for the event. So plan ahead. If you talk about the item, it will sell. Trust me. If you are doing a class on hosting a tea party, make sure you are well stocked in tart servers, tea trays, cookbooks, decorative sugar such as Sugars by Sharon, etc.

Schedule Events Early

Put them on your calendar, put them on your website when you do your regular newsletter and e-zines, let people know what you are doing ahead of time. The sooner you schedule the event, the more opportunities you have to create a "buzz" about it.

Have a "Pay Now" Button

Make sure you put this button on your website for your event. I can't tell you how much of a difference this made when I added the "pay now" option. Many times when customers read your newsletters, e-mails and e-zines, it's after tea room hours. They are in the moment and they want to pay for that event or class now. If they have to wait until tomorrow morning to pay over the phone, they may forget or decide not to spend the money. You need to get their money now and a pay now button takes advantage of those impulse customers.

THE BENEFIT OF PRE-PAY EVENTS

I learned over the years to make all of my paid events pre-pay, non-refundable. This gets the money to you now so you can make preparations. Unfortunately I learned the hard way. Before pre-pay, people would fail to show and I couldn't sell their seat as it was too late at that point. I was out the money I spent on the preparations. It also made me so mad as I had a waiting list of people who wanted to come but last minute notice of availability was too late for them. When I switched to pre-pay events only all of those issues were gone. Of course I always explained our policy over the phone, in person and in writing (on the website). Here is an example of what I did for a Mother's Day Event. It also helps to make the price of the event all-inclusive. Customers actually loved it as they didn't need to mess with bills and money exchange on the day of the event.

On Saturday, May 12 and Sunday, May 13th we will have a special tea in honor of Mother's Day. A special menu will be served. Payment of $34.95 per person (*including* tax and gratuity) will be taken at

> the time the reservation is made. No refunds will be given for cancellations. Please book early for your Mother's Day tea. Space is limited.

Of course there were always exceptions which we had to take on a case by case basis – such as death in the family. I did also let them substitute other people they found to take their place. But if you tell the customer ahead of time as well as publicize it on your e-zines and newsletters, "Before I charge your card, I want to make sure you realize this is a pre-pay event and there are no refunds or cancellations..." there really are very few issues. It makes your life so much easier.

DISCOUNT FOR BOOKING EARLY

Another option we tried with great success was to give them a 10% discount if they booked and paid a month ahead of the event. An example of this wording might be:

> This year, we are offering for the first time, an evening tea on Valentine's Day. In addition to our regular Valentine's Day, we will also be offering a

> special evening time at 6:00. Bring your sweetheart or celebrate a cherished friendship on Saturday, February 14th. Tea Times will be 11 a.m., 1 p.m., 3 p.m. and 6 p.m. This is a special pre-pay event of $37.50 per person (includes tax and gratuity). We will have a special menu tailored around the Valentine's Day festivities. Please book early. No refunds will be given for cancellations. Seating is limited, especially at the 6PM time. You can call the tea room to make your reservations or book on-line at www.afternoontoremember.com. If you pay on-line by January 31st, receive a 10% discount.

Customers love getting a "deal." If they get a discount for booking early, they will.

OTHER KEY STRATEGY IDEAS FOR BOOSTING ATTENDANCE TO YOUR EVENT

Offer Them Food!

Do a tea tasting and offer them free cookies/desserts.

Offer Them Free Recipes/Samples of Tea/Education

Everyone loves getting something for free. People love getting free recipes. Don't worry about "giving your recipe away." They won't go and open their own tea room. On the contrary they'll appreciate how much work it is to make it and they'll come in more often. Many times they just love the idea of "having the recipe." Some of my customers own all of my cookbooks and have never even made any of the recipes. They just like owning them as it gives them a deeper connection to the tea room experience.

Offer Them Fun!

This may sound like a "duh" idea but if you don't say it, they might not think it. Everyone loves fun. Often customers are looking for a little fun in their life or their children's lives and when you specifically advertise, "fun", it calls attention to your event and increases attendance. Anniversary party-games, raffle, prizes all equate to "fun."

Get the Media Involved

Free press is everything! I don't know how many times people told me that and I thought, "I'm sure it is, but how can *I* get it?" If you start getting in the habit of writing/alerting the press for every event you do, eventually they will come to you. I started out by sending them e-mails about my children's events. The media loves children. I would tell them about our Sugar Plum Fairy event and even send them a picture of last year's event. I also would try and tie into the local happenings. In Northern California April is strawberry season and the Strawberry Festival is a big event. I would send in a strawberry scone recipe and a picture of the finished product. Consequently, the local newspaper came out and the writer learned how to make strawberry scones from me. Getting free press does take a bit of patience and persistence, but once you are the "go-to" person for tea in your area, they will call upon you anytime they need someone who knows something about tea. Keep working it even if you feel you aren't making any progress. Often times it helps if you pay to advertise your event in the newspaper/local magazine. Then the next time you have another event, they often work it into an article for free. I've had this happen several times. Also if you refer your business friends to them, they sometimes offer to put you in for free. Persistence and connections are the keys to free press.

Occasionally Offer Free Events

Know your purpose before you decide on a free event, I talked about that previously in Chapter 1 (see page 16), however it's worth repeating. Free events attract new customers.

CHAPTER 3

Know Your Target Audience and Design Events around Them

It's important to know your target audience and design events around them. Of course it's great to experiment with other audiences as well and design events for them, but make sure you know your main audience. Know the ones who spend money at your tea room and keep them happy.

Before you plan an event, think to yourself, "Will this attract my target audience?" If it doesn't, then what is your purpose for the event? Maybe your purpose is to experiment and to entice a new target group, then that's fine. Just always keep your main target audience in mind.

Often times we want to hold an event or teach a class on what we want. Although this may be fun for us, it may not give us the results we are looking for. Remember, it's always about your customer, not about you! You may be tired teaching the same "old" classes, but if that's what your audience wants, then give it to them. However, even a twist on an old event/class can be a great idea. For years I did classes on, "How to Make Scones," and then one day a customer said, "I wish we could just practice making them here." That gave me an idea for a "Hands-On Scone Class." We charged more for this class, could only take 6 participants and were only able to use the kitchen at 7AM. I was a bit skeptical, but can you believe people came for a 7AM class? They did! This was one of our most successful classes and it filled up every time. You just never know. Always keep the customer in mind.

EXPERIMENT WITH OTHER TARGET GROUPS

Even though these groups may not be your "ideal" customer, holding events with these groups in mind, will bring in new customers which will increase your customer base. It may also give your target audience another reason to come in. Designing events for these groups adds spice, new energy and excitement to your tea room.

Children's Events

I know many tea rooms do not cater to children. My tea room was one of them. We started out doing children's birthday parties, but I had too many complaints from regular customers so I stopped doing them. I would reluctantly allow a children's birthday party if they were older and only brought 3 friends or less. Usually, I referred them to other tea rooms in the area that did cater to children and the big birthday parties. However instead of lavish birthday teas, I did hold special children events a few times a year.

Some of our popular ones were the Sugar Plum Fairy Tea held every Friday in December, Alice in Wonderland Tea held during spring break and the Teddy Bear Tea held during summer break. In addition I taught children's etiquette and cooking classes. All of our children's events were always highly publicized so the regular customers (those who did not like the kid atmosphere), did not come on those days. The mothers with children did attend these special children's events and then after they had such a great time with their children, they came back later with their girlfriends during regular tea times. As a result of these children's events, I generated new business by attracting moms looking for activities for their children, and also gaining them as my primary target audience.

Red Hat Groups

Once you do something nice for Red Hat Groups, the word gets out and you'll be the tea room where they want to hold their event.

Working/Non Working Mothers

Providing a speaker with a topic geared toward mothers will bring new customers into your tea room.

Tea Lovers

These are what I call the "pure leaf" people, like myself, not the "afternoon tea" people who favor the tea room experience. Offering topics such as Tea 101 (more later), How to Do a Cupping, and providing guest speakers such as James Norwood Pratt will bring in tea lovers from around the area.

CROSS PROMOTE WITH OTHER INDUSTRIES

I belong to a women's networking group called, "eWomen". I have met so many people through my membership. It was from this group that I learned how valuable cross promoting with other industries can be. We are all in the same "boat". We have the same goal: to increase our customer base and to get people to buy our products and services. It makes perfect sense to cross promote our businesses as long as you can find a way to tie it into your target audience.

In my tea room I had two different life coaches come in and teach a class. I charged for the tea and gave the speaker part of the monies received. The speaker in turn talked to my customers while they were having tea. One life coach talked about balancing your life with family and work and another life coach talked about the empty nest syndrome. Both events were well attended and both speakers gained new clients after the tea. It was a win-win for both of us.

I have also cross promoted with a professional organizer. She came in and taught how to organize your photos and also did another class on, "Organizing Your Clutter". Again, these classes were very successful.

Florists

Have a florist come in and show how to arrange flowers or create a table centerpiece for your tea party.

Spa Services

I have brought my tea treats to their location where they did an open house and offered free/reduced rate spa services and I offered free tea, cookies and desserts. In addition I passed out tea samples and brochures. I gained many customers through these events. I promoted them in my tea room and newsletters and the spa service promoted me to their customers at their location and their newsletter.

Author Events

Author events also work well for cross promoting. If you have a local author in your area, take advantage of this opportunity. It helps you and the author increase business and awareness.

I was fortunate enough to have Babette Donaldson[1], author of the Emma Lea books, in my area. We designed a children's tea around her where she would read her stories, the children would have tea and then she would be available for autographs and pictures after the tea. Often times at these children's events I would demonstrate how easy it is to make tea. I would show the children how to use a tea infuser, how to measure the tea and time the steeping. I also would let one of the children come up and try making tea. This was a very successful event. Not only did I get sales from the tea party itself, but also from the books, tins of tea and accessories I sold. In addition I made it a "pre-pay event" as well.

OTHER IDEAS FOR EXPERIMENTING WITH OTHER TARGET GROUPS

Try hosting meetings for other groups. They

---

[1] http://emmaleabooks.com/

advertise, you advertise and together you increase your customer base. I have held many women's organizational meetings at my tea room. Often times it's nice to offer to provide a short talk on how to make tea, or the history of tea if they hold it at your tea room. Bunco groups, women's church groups and book clubs are all great groups to have at your tea room. Of course you need to be aware of when you schedule these meetings. You shouldn't allow them to have meetings during your busy times, such as Saturdays, or allow them to come in at times when you're not open, such as evenings, unless you think it will benefit you to pay your staff to stay late. Be careful to make sure you think about your needs as well. I have made the mistake of allowing groups to come in after hours and then I had to pay my staff overtime and it wasn't worth it. Make sure it's in your best interest and doesn't cost you extra money. Remember, you are a business and you always need to think about your bottom line.

CHAPTER 4

How to Create Your Own Calendar of Events for the Year

How much should you do? How many events should you have? There is no magic number for events. However, the more you do, the more you offer, the more people will find a reason to visit your tea room. In my opinion you should have no less than one event per month. This does not have to be a "big" event, but you should offer at least something every month whether it be a tea tasting, class, demo or special event.

On the flip side, don't schedule too many events. Know how much you can handle. Don't plan so much that you're stressed out. Space it out evenly. Think about pay days, holidays, what people might be doing, weather, time of year, etc. before you plan your event.

One word of wisdom, don't plan big events when you know your key staff is out of town. As a tea room owner knows, something is bound to happen when you have an event. Perhaps you get sick or your child gets sick. Make sure there will be a key person to handle the event if you can't be there. If you're the only one who can teach a class, you need to train your staff to be able to do it when you can't. You can't be the only one who can do the event. Train and delegate your staff so that you can be gone if you need to.

When planning your calendar of events, start with a calendar, not your iPhone or Blackberry, but a regular paper calendar. Write with pencil and schedule in your events. Think about what days would work best. If Saturday is a high traffic day, then maybe you don't want to plan an event that day. You are already bringing in customers without effort, so plan an event on a day that isn't so popular. Don't take away from your regular crowd. I often chose Thursdays for my classes because of this. After you plan your events on the calendar, look it over and see how it feels. Do you really want to have 3 children's events in one month? Maybe you do, but maybe not. Also have your key staff look it over for things you might have missed. Maybe you planned a big event on a holiday when you're closed. Staff have a way of finding your mistakes and they also think about issues you never even considered, so let them help you.

CHAPTER 5

Ideas to Make Your Event More Memorable

Just as I teach in my "How to Host a Tea Party" classes, there are many ideas which make your event more memorable. This also applies to you, the tea room owner and your events. Details are everything! It's the special attention to detail which make your event memorable so remember the details!

Party Favors

Everyone loves to get something at a party for free. Build the party favors into price of the event. My first anniversary tea, I wanted to make it very special. I gave away a tea starter kit which included a tea sock, samples of tea and a measuring spoon. Everyone was so excited! Other great party favors include: flowers, a small vase, a tea pot ornament, candy dish, tea starter kit, cookie cutter, and/or recipes.

Raffles

Raffles are a great way to increase the energy at the event. It can be as simple as raffling off a gift certificate to a future tea, tins of tea, tea accessories or a basket of tea goodies.

Games

At certain events, it's great to play a game such as Teago[2]. Just be careful that the game doesn't take up too much time as there are some people who are not into games and you want to appeal to everyone.

Contests

If you are having a contest be sure to advertise the contest before the event. A hat contest or tea pot contest are great ideas. It's fun to see who wears the most outrageous hat, or brings in the cutest tea pot or the ugliest tea pot.

---

[2] http://teatimebingo.com/

Take Pictures and Give/Sell Them to Customers

If possible have one of your staff go around and take pictures of the event. Put them up on your website and have customers download them. At my tea room, I purchased a photo printer, took pictures of the tea party, put them in the cute white tea pot frames(from Maryland China[3]) and sold them. This worked well on regular tea days, but during special events, it was difficult to get the photos printed in time before they left the tearoom. Be sure to plan accordingly.

Flowers

Everyone loves flowers. Try tucking a flower into a cute napkin fold at every place setting.

Place Cards

This takes a bit of time to write out everyone's name, but sometimes special events are worth it.

---

[3] http://www.marylandchina.com/

Have Everyone Wear Hats

This can be part of a hat contest as well. Wearing hats breaks down the intimidation of going to tea. It adds to the atmosphere of your event and makes the event fun!

Add a Special Touch to the Everyday

Wrap your chairs with special ribbon for the event or change your table cloths or colors for the event. Even a simple change to the ordinary will make your event more special.

CHAPTER 6

50 Special Event Ideas

Remember you can have an event for any reason. If you are excited about it, your customers will get excited about it. Here are some of our most popular special events.

ANNIVERSARY TEA

My first major event came about as a fluke. I had planned on opening my tea room in the spring but because of permit issues, I didn't actually open until the end of August. Our first year went well. We grew every month until the hot weather hit. Business became extremely slow. I was desperate to have an event to bring in customers, but I couldn't think of anything that would bring in a lot of people during the hot 100 degree Sacramento summer days. Finally it dawned on me to have an anniversary party! Our anniversary was August 27th. I started advertising our event in June. I made it sound like it would be the party of the year. Really, I had no idea what I was doing at the time but sometimes you just need to go with your gut. Because I needed money fast, I decided to do a pre-pay event. Little did I know then, that this would be the start of a great idea. People did pay ahead of time and it helped me get through that first summer. In fact, it was so successful that it became our best event of the year. The anniversary party was a tea buffet with our most popular tea sandwiches, salads, desserts and scones. Our first cookbook also came out that year and we sold a ton of cookbooks at our anniversary party. The next year the party became even bigger and continued the years after that. People even flew in from out of state to attend. Originally we hosted the anniversary party on 2 days but in later years expanded it to 4 days. It was by far the biggest money maker of the year. We had contests, raffles, prizes, party favors and more. It sold out every year. We started out charging $25.00 per person and by the 5th year we ended up charging $47.95 including tax and gratuity. It was the only time of the year that we sat customers together. We sold each ticket as a seat so people who didn't know each other ended up sitting together. They loved it! I still hear comments to this day when I see customers on the street about how great the anniversary party was.

One important idea to remember about successful events, it's critical to document everything you did after the fact. Write down where you advertised, what you did, how many you served, and what you served. I didn't do that the first year. The second year, I made notes about everything: how much food we prepared, how much was left over, how many customers, how many staff were on-hand, which seatings sold out first, etc. This helped me so much the next year. Be sure to keep careful notes. It makes it so much easier and you don't end up recreating "the wheel," every year. You know what worked and what didn't. And even though you think you will never forget, you will. Write it down!

CHILDREN'S EVENTS

This can be a big category if you are into children's teas. Even if you are not, try hosting a few throughout the year to bring in new target groups. Here are a few that I did in my tea room.

Sugar Plum Fairy Tea

This event was held every Friday late afternoon in December. It was about an hour long event. Children dressed up in their finest attire. We offered seasonal treats, scones and a decaffeinated tea. I usually read a story such as, "The Night Before Christmas." The highlight for the children was a visit from Santa. We were fortunate to have a fire station near our tea room. One of the men dressed up as Santa and arrived on the fire truck during the last part of the tea. The fire men came and passed out candy bags to all of the children. Everyone had a great time! Originally the first year we offered this event only once in December, but it quickly became so popular that the next year we did it every Friday in December.

Alice in Wonderland Tea

This tea was offered during spring break. It too lasted about an hour. I dressed up as Alice and my son dressed in a bunny costume. For this event, I usually taught a quick class on manners and etiquette. I also taught the children how to set a proper table and even had volunteers come up and practice setting it with me. We talked about using milk and sugar in tea. I even had my son demonstrate how easy it is to make tea. We served child-focused tea food such as cute peanut butter sandwiches cut out in tea pot shapes. The mothers loved bringing their children to this event as it gave them something fun to do during spring break.

OTHER FUN TEAS FOR CHILDREN

Mother/Daughter Tea

This is a great tea to do during the month of May. Mothers love doing special things with their daughters.

Father/Daughter Tea

This tea wasn't as popular, but depending on your area, and what you do during the tea, this could be a great event.

Children's Cooking Classes

Some ideas are "How to Make Tea

Sandwiches" and "How to Decorate Tea Cookies". Just remember to keep the classes short and simple.

Miss Spider's Tea Party

You can take practically any children's book and turn it into a book-based tea party. Have the children dress up as characters of the book and then have someone read the story. Miss Spider's Tea Party was held around Halloween and the children dressed in their Halloween costumes. I read the story and we served Halloween themed tea treats such as pumpkin cookies, monster fingers, etc.

Lady Bug's Tea Party

This was another one of those events and was held in the summer. We used green checkered plastic table cloths I found at a discount store and served picnic tea food. The children created and decorated their own lady bug out of construction paper to take home.

Children's Teddy Bear Tea

This event was also held in the summer.

Children brought in their own teddies for tea. I talked about manners and etiquette at this tea as well. We served tea themed food such as brownies decorated with Gummibears. At the end I passed out a handout on manners. Below is an example:

A Few Tips on Children's Table Etiquette

1. Always use your fork, unless the food is meant to be eaten with your fingers.
2. Don't stuff your mouth full of food.
3. Chew with your mouth closed and don't talk with your mouth full.
4. Be careful what you say about the food, it could hurt someone's feelings.
5. Always say thank you when served.
6. Wait until everyone is seated and served before eating.
7. Eat slowly, don't gobble.
8. When eating rolls, bread, or scones, break off a piece before buttering. Eating the whole piece doesn't look nice.
9. Politely ask for someone to pass the food instead of reaching across.
10. Always dab your napkin to your mouth. Don't use your sleeve. Keep your napkin in your lap.

11. If you need to blow your nose, do it in the bathroom.
12. Always thank your host even if you didn't like the food.

Parents loved it when I went over this sheet. Plus it was a fun environment for the children to learn, reinforce manners and practice proper etiquette.

TIPS ON PLANNING A CHILDREN'S EVENT

When you are planning a children's tea, remember to keep it short and sweet. You may be appealing to a wide variety of ages so keep things moving. Have a set agenda and stick to it. Don't seat everyone until the start time. It's tempting but if you do, the children get bored, want food immediately and the parents feel as if they had to sit for a long time. If they arrived early, we would say, "Our children's tea doesn't start until 3:00. You are welcome to look around in our gift shop, or take a walk outside. We will be seating right at 3:00." Another good tip is to announce to the children the order of events. For example on the Sugar Plum Fairy tea, I would say, "First we will read a story, next we will enjoy some delicious goodies and then we'll have a special surprise." Children do better when they know what's expected of them. Parents were always amazed how great their children did at our events. They sat quietly, listened and had a fantastic time. The trick is to have a set agenda, tell them the agenda, keep it moving and have fun!

CLASSES AS EVENTS

Classes make excellent events. Customers love to learn what you do from cooking to napkin folding. The primary target audience for my tea room were ladies in their 40's and up. Most often these women had free time to attend a class. We did classes on everything! We even did a class and tea on "Highlights of the World Tea Expo", one year. They wanted to know all about the expo, so I decided to have a class on it. I charged for the class and tea treats. We sat around tables and had tea while I explained what I had learned, the people I had met and the teas I tasted. Everyone had fun!

Cooking classes are very popular. If you

publish your own cookbook, this is definitely the marketing tool for you! Below are some of our most popular cooking classes.

How to Make Scones Class

This was by far our most popular cooking class and still is. You can do separate classes for different varieties of scones. During February I did a class on Chocolate Raspberry Scones and in the fall I did a class on Pumpkin Pecan Scones. Even though the tea room is no longer open, I still teach these classes at the Antique Trove where I have a boutique booth. When it was at the tea room, I charged about $24.95 and it included a small afternoon tea in addition to the class. For the tea room class, I passed out the recipe, showed them how to make the scones, went over tips and then we enjoyed the tea together while I answered questions. For the Antique Trove, I do not charge for the class as I want to attract the people already in the store and I don't have kitchen facilities there to serve tea. However, I do not give out the recipe in this class, but rather tips on making scones. That way, the customers buy my cookbooks if they want the recipes. It's a win-win for both of us. The customers get free information and I get their sales from my cookbooks. This is also another example of a free event which benefits both parties.

How to Make Tea Sandwiches

This is also a popular class. There really are tricks to making perfect tea sandwiches. Remember, you are the expert. What you think is simple, may not be to your customers. They love to hear ideas for fillings, garnishes, storing and serving ideas. I pass out a tips sheet on this class as well. After the class we enjoy sampling the different kinds of sandwiches.

How to Host a Holiday Tea Party

In this class I talked about tea foods you could prepare ahead of time, how to decorate your table on a budget, party favors and menu ideas. I passed out tips to a successful tea party as well as recipes.

How to Host a Spring Tea Party

This was a similar class to the one above but for

a different season. In this class I focused on wedding/baby showers as well.

How to Make Quiche

It's amazing how many people do not really cook anymore. That is one of the reasons I started teaching cooking classes. Customers loved our quiche, but many had never made one. So this class was born. Customers love watching you in action, so show them what you do!

OTHER IDEAS FOR CLASSES

How to Make Lemon Curd and Devonshire Cream

My customers could not get enough of these condiments. They were eager to learn how to make them.

How to Make Homemade Soup

We had great soups and customers enjoyed learning how they could make them at home.

How to Plan a Wedding Shower Tea

Many people are scared to do large events. By giving them a few tips, you can give them the confidence they need. This class can also be a big money maker for your gift items and loose tea sales.

How to Make Decorative Sugar

This was a wild idea for my sugar lady, Sugars By Sharon[4]. I know she was a bit nervous and thought I was nuts that I would teach a class on how to make sugar. However, trusting what I knew about giving away my recipes, I knew customers would end up buying more of her sugar than actually making it on their own. So I showed them how to make it with a recipe I had found. While making the sugar, I talked about how Sharon had custom-designed molds, how perfect her packaging was and how in awe I was of what she actually did. Making sugar is tedious. There is definitely an art to it. Yes, you can make sugar for your bridal shower but when you want a nice gift to give someone,

---

[4] http://www.sugarsbysharon.com/

chances are you will just buy a package of her sugar. My objective for this class was not to really "teach" customers how to make sugar, but rather to get everyone excited about decorative sugar. After teaching the class, by the end of the month I had sold all of the sugar I had bought from Sharon. Customers love new activities and excitement. Plus they appreciate what you do when you share it with them. Don't worry about sharing your "secret," or "giving your recipe away." They will come back to you because they value what you do.

TEA TASTINGS AND CLASSES AS EVENTS

Tea tastings make great informal or formal events. You can do a special tasting when the first flush spring tea arrives or a special holiday tasting of the flavored black teas. In the summer you can hold an iced tea tasting and health benefits of tea class.

Tea Classes

You can also break your tea classes up according to levels. I taught 3 tea classes. Tea 101 which were the basics of tea, Tea 102 which were black teas from India, China and Sri Lanka and the Tea 103 class which were oolong teas. In each class I explained the processing method, we examined the tea leaves and then tasted 3-6 different teas. For the special classes, I would limit the class size to just 6 students but charge more (pre-pay event only). In these classes the students prepared their own tea with a tasting set, then we discussed and took notes on the tea. At the end, most students bought tea.

Tea Tasting Ideas

Taste a tea that complements the season. Fall is great for teas that are pumpkin or spice flavored. Spring is a great time for a new Darjeeling. Summer could be for excellent iced teas with a recipe to hand out such as this one:

Gourmet Iced Tea

To brew approximately 2 quarts of gourmet iced tea with loose tea leaves:

Use fresh, cold water from the tap or spring water. Do not reuse water you have already boiled since the oxygen will have evaporated and this affects the taste of the tea.

Measure ¼ cup of tea leaves (to make 2 quarts or 8 cups) into your infuser. For this quantity of leaves, you will need a large infuser for the leaves to have room to expand and brew properly. A cotton tea sock large basket infuser or the paper tea filters will work perfectly. Use a tea pot to house the infuser and brew the tea.

Heat 4 cups of water until it reaches the correct temperature: generally, about 180° for green, greener oolongs and almost a full boil for black teas, blacker oolongs, herbal infusions and fruit blends. Pour it over the leaves immediately and cover your teapot.

Brew the tea for 5 minutes for black teas, 2-3 minutes for green and 7-10 minutes for Rooibos or herbal teas. Over brewing can cause the tea to taste bitter so use the appropriate time according to the specific tea.

After brewing, remove the leaves immediately.

> Fill a 2 quart pitcher with ice. Pour the tea over the ice and into the pitcher and sweeten if desired. Then, add enough cold tap water to fill the pitcher. This will make a strong tea, you can dilute with more water according to your tastes.
>
> A 4oz. tin makes about 14 quarts
>
> A 2 oz. tin makes about 7 quarts

Tea Tastings

Do tastings to highlight the differences in teas: whites, greens, oolongs, blacks, flavored teas, herbals and tisanes.

Health Benefits of Tea

This is a great class to do in January after the holidays when everyone is dieting.

Iced Tea Tastings

Do this as a separate tasting with teas that are great iced.

OTHER SPECIAL EVENT IDEAS

April Fool's Tea

This is a cute idea I received from a customer. Have this tea on April 1st and use dishes and tea themed foods from all seasons, Christmas, Halloween, etc.

Special Guests

Invite famous locals from your city and have a tea for them. I was fortunate enough to have James Norwood Pratt come to my tea room twice. What an honor!

History of Afternoon Tea

There are so many customers enthralled with the history of tea. Give them the basics. James Norwood Pratt's book on the New Tea Lover's Treasury and Jane Pettigrew's book on The Social History of Tea are perfect references for you as well as other authors.

Start a book club!

Start a book club and charge for the tea. Use

the murder mystery tea books such as the Laura Child's books or any book you would like. Meet once a month.

Empty Nester's Tea

Have a life coach, counselor or therapist come in and talk about the adjustments when the children leave home. I was amazed how popular this tea event was at my tea room!

How to Make Gift Baskets

Have someone come in and show your customers how to make a tea gift basket. Serve them tea and scones.

MIX IT UP!

Even a twist on an old event can be a great idea! Look how many events you can do for Valentine's Day!

Valentine's Day Tea

This can be a traditional themed tea held at regular tea times for friends to celebrate the occasion.

Valentine's Evening Tea

I was a bit reluctant to give up my Valentine's evening with my husband for this event, but this tea was so popular and it gave the customers a real "reason" to bring their husbands in for tea. Women always want to share the tea experience with their husbands, but husbands are often reluctant to come in. Valentine's evening tea is the perfect Valentine's gift to their wives.

How to Host Your Own Valentine's Day Tea

Give your customers ideas for hosting their own Valentine's Day party. Teach a class on how to decorate, what to serve and tea suggestions.

Now you can see how many events you can host just from Valentine's Day. It's all the same holiday but 3 different events for 3 different audiences.

ABOVE ALL, HAVE FUN!

Whatever event you do, make sure you have fun. If you are excited about it, your enthusiasm will be contagious and spread to your staff and your customers. Excitement builds good business and makes for great events! Good business and events bring in customers for life!

ABOUT THE AUTHOR

Amy Lawrence is an example for women who have had many successful careers in life, including teacher and business owner. With a master's degree in Special Education, she taught for 11 years. In 2003 she decided to pursue her passion and opened her tea room, An Afternoon to Remember. It won many awards including Best Small Tea Room in the U.S. in 2006, KCRA's A-List in 2007, 2008 and 2009, and Sacramento Magazine's Best Tea Room in 2008. In 2009, Amy closed her tea room in order to devote herself full-time to her family and other companies: Afternoon to Remember Fine Tea and Gifts and ATR Publishing. Amy has published eight cookbooks and sold more than 10,000 of them. She is currently working on several new projects, including resources for new tea room owners.

Also from ATR Publishing

Creating an Afternoon to Remember

A Little of This and a Little of That

Making It Your Own Afternoon to Remember

Tea Time Tidbits and Treats

Drop by for Tea

Master Tea Room Recipes

**Order them online at
http://www.afternoontoremember.com/**

www.ingramcontent.com/pod-product-compliance
Lightning Source LLC
Chambersburg PA
CBHW051715040426
42446CB00008B/889